This book belongs to:

____

Made in the USA
Monee, IL
23 April 2021

66567724R00066